HIGH-STAKES HEISTS

BANK HEISTS

KENNY ABDO

Fly!
An Imprint of Abdo Zoom
abdobooks.com

abdobooks.com

Published by Abdo Zoom, a division of ABDO, P.O. Box 398166, Minneapolis, Minnesota 55439. Copyright © 2025 by Abdo Consulting Group, Inc. International copyrights reserved in all countries. No part of this book may be reproduced in any form without written permission from the publisher. Fly!™ is a trademark and logo of Abdo Zoom.

Printed in the United States of America, North Mankato, Minnesota.
052024
092024

 THIS BOOK CONTAINS RECYCLED MATERIALS

Photo Credits: Alamy, AP Images, Getty Images, Granger Collection, Shutterstock
Production Contributors: Kenny Abdo, Jennie Forsberg, Grace Hansen
Design Contributors: Candice Keimig, Neil Klinepier

Library of Congress Control Number: 2023948546

Publisher's Cataloging-in-Publication Data

Names: Abdo, Kenny, author.
Title: Bank heists / by Kenny Abdo
Description: Minneapolis, Minnesota : Abdo Zoom, 2025 | Series: High-stakes heists | Includes online resources and index.
Identifiers: ISBN 9781098285708 (lib. bdg.) | ISBN 9781098286408 (ebook) | ISBN 9781098286750 (Read-to-me eBook)
Subjects: LCSH: Theft--Juvenile literature. | Bank robberies--Juvenile literature. | Banks and banking--Juvenile literature. | Stealing--Juvenile literature. | Robbery--Juvenile literature.
Classification: DDC 364.162--dc23

TABLE OF CONTENTS

Bank Heists 4

The Plotting 6

The Scores 10

The Getaway 20

Glossary 22

Online Resources 23

Index 24

BANK HEISTS

As long as banks have been around, there have been people lurking around the corner planning the perfect heist to empty them!

THE PLOTTING

Banking can be traced back to around 2000 BCE. The 17th and 18th centuries saw the growth of banking in Europe. Banking reached the United States in 1784.

It wasn't long until the first heist was hatched. In 1831, two men walked away with $245,000 from the Bank of New York. After that, many robbers have walked out of banks with other people's money.

THE SCORES

The Great Brink's Robbery happened in 1950. It was called "the Crime of the Century." Eight people got life sentences for the heist. But less than $60,000 of the $2 million stolen was ever recovered.

In 1972, six thieves robbed a bank in California. They heard President Richard Nixon had a **slush fund** there. They slipped away with $30 million. The robbers were eventually caught.

Valerio Viccei almost pulled off the perfect crime in 1987. He broke into a London bank, stole millions, and **fled** to South America. Viccei was finally arrested when he returned to England and was sentenced to 22 years of hard time.

In 1997, six men robbed the Dunbar Armored transportation company's vault. They almost got away with nearly $19 million. However, one robber lent some of the stolen cash to a friend, but forgot to remove the original **bank straps**!

Saddam Hussein arranged the largest bank heist in history. Before the **Iraq War** began in 2003, he stole $1 billion from the Central Bank of Iraq. Only $650 million was recovered. The rest may never be found.

In 2005, a 25-member gang dug a tunnel under Banco Central in Brazil. They stole the **equivalent** of $32 million in **Brazilian real**. Only eight of the 25 were arrested, while just $4 million was recovered.

The largest cash robbery in British history happened in 2006. Masked men kidnapped a branch manager and held his family hostage. They made off with the **equivalent** of $17 million. The makeup artist who designed the masks helped the police catch the men.

An elderly gentleman posed as a wealthy jewel dealer in 2006. He befriended the staff of ABN Bank by giving them chocolates. While the staff was distracted, the thief walked off with $28 million!

In 2015, six elderly English thieves **plotted** their last heist. They took the **equivalent** of $17 million from an underground safe deposit facility in London. Eventually, they were all arrested and sentenced in 2016.

THE GETAWAY

Banks are important when it comes to people saving for their future. And thankfully, some of the thieves who have **plotted** to take that away have been held accountable!

GLOSSARY

banking – the business conducted or services offered by a bank.

bank straps – or currency strap, a simple paper device designed to hold a specific denomination and number of banknotes.

Brazilian real – the official currency of Brazil.

equivalent – when two things are the same in amount or value.

flee – to quickly run away or escape.

Iraq War – a conflict that began in March 2003 when the United States and its allies invaded Iraq. After the fall of the Iraqi government, US troops remained in Iraq to help stabilize the new government.

plot – to secretly make plans to carry out an illegal action.

slush fund – money used for unlawful purposes like political bribery.

ONLINE RESOURCES

Booklinks
NONFICTION NETWORK
FREE! ONLINE NONFICTION RESOURCES

To learn more about bank heists, please visit **abdobooklinks.com** or scan this QR code. These links are routinely monitored and updated to provide the most current information available.

INDEX

ABN Amro Bank Heist 18

Banco Central Burglary 16

Bank of New York 9

Dunbar Armored Robbery 14

Great Brink's Robbery 10

Hatton Garden Safe Deposit Burglary 19

Hussein, Saddam 15

Iraq War 15

Knightsbridge Security Deposit Robbery 12

Nixon, Richard 11

Securitas Depot Robbery 17

Viccei, Valerio 12